Three Degrees of Glory

A Discourse on God's Plan and Blessings;
Human Happiness and Spiritual Joy in
Life and in Afterlife

By Melvin Joseph Ballard

Published by Pantianos Classics

ISBN-13: 978-1-78987-256-9

First published in 1922

Contents

The Three Degrees of Glory

This is an inspiring sight, a convincing testimony of your interest in this great and important feature of the latter-day work. I rejoice with you to live in this wonderful day, the most glorious and splendid that has ever dawned in the history of man. I am exceedingly happy to be here tonight in your presence to rejoice with you on this ninety-ninth anniversary of the appearance of the Angel Moroni to the Prophet Joseph Smith, for it was just ninety-nine years ago tonight that Moroni spent the entire night unfolding to the prophet the greatness of this latter-day dispensation and explaining to him for the first time, in this dispensation at least, the meaning of the promise that Elijah, the prophet, should come again to turn the hearts of the fathers to the children and those of the children to the fathers lest the whole earth should be smitten with a curse. I know of no more fitting way to celebrate that wonderful event in this dispensation than to be here discussing this subject. I rejoice because to us has been given the most splendid revelations God has ever given to man, and this is not discrediting anything of the past. It is full of glory, full of inspiration and grandeur, full of majesty and of truth!

The greatest revelation the Lord, Jesus Christ, has ever given to man, so far as a record is made, was given to the Prophet Joseph Smith on the 16th of April, 1832, known as the 76th section of the book of Doctrine & Covenants, commonly called for years and still known as "The Vision." This to my mind is the climax of all wonderful revelations that have come from the Lord from the days of Father Adam until the present moment.

Men have been groping in darkness on some subjects, even in gospel dispensations of the past. They have not known the fulness of God's plan and purpose for the salvation of his sons and daughters, but surely this is a glorious time, for this is the Dispensation of the Fulness of Times, and all that men have ever had in all former dispensations has been given at once in this dispensation, and much that was not had in other dispensations. How wonderful it is to live now, when we are not in doubt concerning not only ourselves, but the whole scheme and plan of salvation, not only for the living, but also for the dead.

Men have been speculating as to God's provisions for the salvation of his children. There have been those in the past and some still remain who teach that if by the smallest margin one fails to meet the conditions of the gospel they lose eternal salvation and are eternally damned; and on the other hand, there are those who believe that certain individuals are marked and designated, predestined, to come into this life to be saved no matter what they do, and others to be eternally lost. There are those who are so narrow as to believe that if in this life men have not found the Way, the Light, and Truth, there is no hope for them beyond the grave. I rejoice to live-when the fulness of truth has been given and when an answer has been made clearly and definitely in the word of the Lord to all queries on this subject.

Your minds and hearts are set upon knowing what you must do to obtain the greatest thing the Lord has offered. I want to talk about that more than anything else because I do not discover many of you who would be satisfied with second-hand things, and you are not contented or happy by having second best or third best. So we will begin by reading a description of the terms and conditions that we must comply with to obtain the celestial glory. I think it will be worth every sacrifice required and a hundred times more if need be. Personally, I would give it to attain that which God has offered to men and women who enter into the celestial glory.

WE read in the Doctrine & Covenants: "They are they who received the testimony of Jesus, and believed on his name and were baptized after the manner of his burial, being buried in the water in his name, and this according to the commandment which he has given." (D. & C. 76:51.)

I now say to all the world that no man, no woman, ever shall see the celestial kingdom of God who is not baptized of the water and of the spirit. The Lord has specified it. He made it so binding and complete when after announcing the law he complied with every term himself, though perfect, so that no man who imagines himself to be perfect here can excuse himself or herself from obedience to the law of baptism. It is the door, the gate to Celestial Glory.

"That by keeping the commandments they might be washed and cleansed from all their sins, and receive the Holy Spirit by the laying on of the hands of him who is ordained and sealed unto this power;

"And who overcome by faith, and are sealed by the Holy Spirit of promise, which the Father sheds forth upon all those who are just and true."(Ibid.: 52-53.)

I would like to pause and emphasize that passage, because, while we receive eternal blessings at the hands of the priesthood which has the right to seal on earth and it shall be sealed in heaven, this revelation clearly states it must be sealed by the holy spirit of promise also.

A man and woman may by fraud and deception obtain admittance to the house of the Lord and may receive the pronouncement of the Holy Priesthood, giving to them, so far as lies in their power, these blessings. We may deceive men, but we cannot deceive the Holy Ghost, and our blessings will not be eternal unless they are also sealed by the holy spirit of promise, the Holy Ghost, one who reads the thoughts and hearts of men and gives his sealing approval to the blessings pronounced upon their heads. Then it is binding, efficacious, and of full force.

I thank the Lord that there is this provision, so that even though men are able to deceive their brethren, they are not able to deceive the Holy Ghost and thus come into possession of their blessings unless they prove in word, in thought, and in deed their worthiness and righteousness.

Reading again from the 53rd verse:

"And who overcome by faith, and are sealed by the Holy Spirit of promise, which the Father sheds forth upon all those who are just and true.

"They are they who are the church of the Firstborn.

"They are they into whose hands the Father has given all things-"(Ibid. 53-55.)

Is there anything that you have ever dreamed of that you wanted, that you longed for? Into the hands of those who attain this glory shall all things be given.

What a world of meaning! You can ponder over that all the rest of your lives and every thought and aspiration of the human heart in righteousness that it is possible for men to conceive will be but a fraction of that which is comprehended in this statement, that "Unto them shall be given all things," because it is not possible for mortals to think of a thousandth part of what this means.

Reading again:

"They are they who are priests and kings, who have received of his fulness, and of his glory.

"And are priests of the Most High, after the order of Melchizedek, which was after the order of Enoch, which was after the order of the Only Begotten Son.

"Wherefore, as it is written, they are gods, even the sons of God-" (Ibid. 57-58.)

WE HAVE frequently said that perhaps the grandest thought that has ever been brought forth to the children of men is the Mormon truism, namely: "As man is, God once was, and as God is, man may become." The foundation of that truism is in this revelation and these words we have just read. Let me read them again:

"Wherefore, as it is written, they are gods, even the sons of God-"

Now, I would like to say a word or two about that Mormon truism, namely: "As man is, God once was, and as God is, man may become."

Note that it is not to the effect that man will become, but man may become, and I wish to say that few men will become what God is. And yet, all men may become what he is if they will pay the price.

Now, I wish to say to you that the only possible candidates to become what God is are those who attain celestial glory, and those who fail in that will never, worlds without end, be possible candidates to become what God is. Then I wish to say to you that there are three degrees of glory in the celestial kingdom and only those who attain the highest degree of celestial glory will be candidates to become what God is, and graduate.

So you see, it is within the reach of every man and woman who lives, but only attainable by those who pay the price, who stand the test, who prove themselves, who comply with the terms and conditions that make their calling and election sure.

I wish now just a moment to diverge and turn to the 131st section of the book of Doctrine & Convenants. It is very brief and is upon the point I am just discussing. It is a revelation which was given May 16th and May 17th, 1843.

In the celestial glory there are three heavens or degrees:

"And in order to obtain the highest, a man must enter into this order of the priesthood, (meaning the new and everlasting covenant of marriage);

"And if he does not, he cannot obtain it.

"He may enter into the other, but that is the end of his kingdom; he cannot have an increase." (Ibid. 131:1-4.)

Those who are denied endless increase cannot be what God is because that, in connection with other things, makes him God. The eternity of the marriage convenant ought to be understood by Latter-day Saints clearly to be the sealing of at least one woman to one man for time and for all eternity. Then do not get confused on that point and imagine that it necessarily means more than one woman. It may be, certainly, but it does mean at least that one man and one woman are sealed together by the power of the Holy Priesthood and by the sealing approval of the Holy Ghost for time and for all eternity, and then that they keep their convenants, before they will be candidates for the highest degree of celestial glory, and unto them only of all these groups of our Father's children is the promise made of endless or eternal increase.

What do we mean by endless or eternal increase? We mean that through the righteousness and faithfulness of men and women who keep the commandments of God they will come forth with celestial bodies, fitted and prepared to enter into their great, high and eternal glory in the celestial kingdom of God; and unto them, through their preparation, there will come children, who will be spirit children. I don't think that is very difficult to comprehend and understand. The nature of the offspring is determined by the nature of the substance that flows in the veins of the being. When blood flows in the veins of the being, the offspring will be what blood produces, which is tangible flesh and bone, but when that which flows in the veins is spirit matter, a substance which is more refined and pure and glorious than blood, the offspring of such beings will be spirit children. By that I mean they will be in

9

the image of the parents. They will have a spirit body and have a spark of the eternal or divine that always did exist in them.

Unto such parentage will this glorious privilege come, for it is written in our scriptures that "the glory of God is to bring to pass the immortality and eternal life of man." So, it will be the glory of men and women that will make their glory like unto his. When the power of endless increase shall come to them, and their offspring, growing and multiplying through ages that shall come, they will be in due time, as we have been, provided with an earth like this, wherein they too may obtain earthly bodies and pass through all the experiences through which we have passed, and then we shall hold our relationship to them, the fulness and completeness of which has not been revealed to us, but we shall stand in our relationship to them as God, our Eternal Father, does to us, and thereby is this the most glorious and wonderful privilege that ever will come to any of the sons and daughters of God.

Now I wish to return to the 76th section: "Wherefore, all things are theirs, whether life or death, or things present, or things to come, all are theirs and they are Christ's and Christ is God's.

"And they shall overcome all things." (Ibid. 59-60.)

Here is a significant statement. I have said that in addition to one's baptism of the water and of the spirit, which is essential for admission to the kingdom of God, we are to add to our faith virtue, to virtue knowledge, to knowledge temperance, patience, brotherly kindness, godliness, humility, and diligence. If these things be not in us, we are blind and cannot see afar, but if they are in us, they will make us so that we will be able to make our calling and election sure.

A man may receive the priesthood and all its privileges and blessings, but until he learns to overcome the flesh, his temper, his tongue, his disposition to indulge in the things God has forbidden, he cannot come into the celestial kingdom of God-he must overcome either in this life or in the life to come. But this life is the time in which men are to repent. Do not let any of us imagine that we can go down to the grave not having overcome the corruptions of the flesh and then lose in the grave all our sins and evil tendencies. They will be with us. They will be with the spirit when separated from the body.

It is my judgment that any man or woman can do more to conform to the laws of God in one year in this life than they could in ten years when they are dead. The spirit only can repent and change, and then the battle has to go forward with the flesh afterwards. It is much easier to overcome and serve the Lord when both flesh and spirit are combined as one. This is the time when men are more pliable and susceptible. When clay is pliable, it is much easier to change than when it gets hard and sets.

This life is the time to repent. That is why I presume it will take a thousand years after the first resurrection until the last group will be prepared to come forth. It will take them a thousand years to do what it would have taken, but three score years and ten to accomplish in this life.

You remember the vision of the redemption of the dead as given to the Church through the late President Joseph F. Smith. President Smith saw the spirits of the righteous dead after their resurrection, and the language is the same as the one of the Prophet Joseph's revelations-that they, the righteous dead, looked upon the absence of their spirits from their bodies as a bondage.

I grant you that the righteous dead will be at peace, but I tell you that when we go out of this life, leave this body, we will desire to do many things that we cannot do at all without the body. We will be seriously handicapped, and we will long for the body; we will pray for that early reunion with our bodies. We will know then what advantage it is to have a body.

Then every man and woman who is putting off until the next life the task of correcting and overcoming the weakness of the flesh are sentencing themselves to years of bondage, for no man or woman will come forth in the resurrection until he has completed his work, until he has overcome, until he has done as much as he can do. That is why Jesus said in the resurrection there is neither marriage or giving in marriage, for all such contracts-agreements-will be provided for those who are worthy of it before men and women come forth in the resurrection, and those who are complying in this life with these conditions are shortening their sentences, for every one of us will have a matter of years in that spirit state to complete and finish our salvation. And some may attain, by reason of their righteousness in this life, the right to do postgraduate work, to be admitted into the celestial kingdom, but others will lose absolutely the right to that glory, all they can do will not avail after death to bring them into the celestial kingdom.

The point I have in mind is that we are sentencing ourselves to long periods of bondage, separating our spirits from our bodies, or we are shortening that period, according to the way in which we overcome and master ourselves.

"Wherefore, let no man glory in man, but rather let him glory in God, who shall subdue all enemies under his feet.

"These shall dwell in the presence of God and his Christ forever and ever." (Ibid. 61-62.)

Do you comprehend it, you who gain celestial glory, the privilege of dwelling in the presence of God and his Christ forever and ever? What did it mean to have in the world, during his ministry, for three brief years the Lord Jesus Christ-not the Father, just the Son? It was the most wonderful privilege the world has ever had. What would you give tonight for the privilege of standing in the presence of the Son for five minutes? You would give all your earthly possessions for that privilege. Then can you comprehend the full meaning and significance of the statement that those who gain celestial glory will have the privilege of dwelling in the presence of the Father and the Son forever and ever? That, in itself, will be reward enough for the struggle to obtain the prize. Yea, it is beyond price and earthly possessions. Even the giving of life itself would be a trifle for the privilege to dwell forever and ever in the presence of the Father and the Son.

NOW I want to make an explanation that you may comprehend and understand God's plan, which allows us to dwell in his presence. The Lord has created by and through his Son, Jesus Christ, according to the book of Moses, worlds without number, and numerous are they as the sands upon the seashore. In each one, undoubtedly, dwells a group of his children. Then how can he dwell in the presence of all these several groups at one and the same time? If you will read the 88th section of Doctrine & Covenants, toward the latter part of that section the Lord undertakes to explain it.

The Lord told Joseph Smith how he looks upon these, his kingdoms, worlds without number, and he said, "I know them. I count them." And Moses wondered and wanted to know about them. But the Lord said unto Moses, "Only an account of this earth give I unto you."

There is something else to learn after we leave this earth, and I rejoice in the anticipation of further and greater knowledge concerning the things I do not now understand and comprehend. The Lord touched Joseph's understanding when he said, Behold, these are known to me. They are like a man having a field, and he sent a group of workers to this part of the field and gave them instructions what to do and told them he would visit them in their hour and in their time. He sent out the second group into another part of the field, and another group, and unto each of them he made the promise that he would visit them in their hour and in their time and season until they all would be made glad by the joy of his countenance. He would visit them from the first to the last and from the last to the first in one eternal round, each in his time, in his hour and in his season.

I presume that is the reason that the promise is made that Christ will dwell with men on this earth for a thousand years and that will be our day, our time, and then I presume he will do as suggested in this 88th section; he will visit other places and kingdoms; but while absent from this group we will, nevertheless, be in his presence, in communication with him.

Every man and woman who enters the celestial kingdom will find themselves living on this earth, which shall be a celestial world, and we will identify it as the earth upon which we have lived. Each man and woman who enters that kingdom will find the earth a Urim and Thummim, looking into which one may learn about all conditions and kingdoms that are beneath and the kingdom in which we live, so that all depths are revealed to us.

The revelations referred to inform us that whosoever enters the celestial kingdom shall receive a white stone, a Urim and Thummim of greatest purity. Through the gift and power of God it will enable the possessor to read the universe and obtain knowledge from all kingdoms, not only the one in which we dwell, so that we will comprehend all heights and all depths. Those who gain celestial glory, to them only comes this privilege, and though absent it is possible for the Father and the Son to commune and converse with all who are entitled to enjoy that companionship, the other Comforter, just as the Holy Ghost now has the right and power to operate and converse at once with ten thousand or ten million souls who have complied with baptism and have been brought within the circle in tune that they may receive the communication. Every man and woman will hear at once and dwell in his presence to be constantly instructed.

I ought not to spend any time trying to persuade you that this is possible when you know that in this day the human voice has been magnified a hundred thousand times by the skill of man, so that it is said the human voice may be increased one hundred thousand times and encircle the globe. If we can do that, and we do it every day, what does God know about it? So much more than we know and comprehend that our advances are just a feeble opening of the great eternal truths of science and knowledge which God has.

I understand now something about that wonderful appearance of the Redeemer to the Nephites. They heard a voice, and though it was not a loud voice and came from the clouds, yet it was a keen and penetrating voice so that it entered every heart and made their very frames quake. Now I understand that God knows how. Though absent, he may speak, and all the groups of his children who are entitled to hear him, shall hear, and in their hour and in their time and season enjoy his personal presence and forever and always his companionship, the companionship of his spirit and his personal ministry through his means of communication with such souls.

I cannot begin this night to tell you what that means-to enjoy the blessings and privileges of dwelling in Christ's presence forever and ever. I know how the soul is thrilled; I know the feeling that comes by being in his presence for but a moment. I would give all that I am, all that I hope to be, to have the joy of his presence, to dwell in his love and his affection and to be in favor with the Master of all things forever and ever.

I wish now to call your attention to other revelations which the Lord has given in this dispensation relative to those who have died without law.

You will recall how the Prophet Joseph was greatly concerned over his own Brother Alvin. Alvin Smith was a devout believer in Joseph's vision, but prior to the restoration of the priesthood and the restoration of the doctrine of baptism, he died. Joseph was deeply concerned over his death, and the Lord gave Joseph Smith a revelation, wherein he said he saw Alvin in the celestial kingdom. Alvin was not really there; it was Alvin's right and privilege to be there; but he could not go there without baptism. The Lord said all who would have received the gospel had they heard it, they too will be candidates for the celestial glory. Who are they? How can they be determined?

Some folk get the notion that the problems of life will at once clear up, and they will know that this is the gospel of Christ when they die. I have heard people say they believe when they die, they will see Peter and that he will clear it all up. I said, "You never will see Peter until you accept the gospel of the Lord Jesus Christ, at the hands of the elders of the Church, living or dead. They will meet these men to whom this right and authority has been given, for this generation shall receive it at the hands of those who have been honored with the priesthood of this dispensation. Living or dead, they shall not hear it from anyone else."

So, men won't know any more when they are dead than when they are living, only they will have passed through the change called death. They will not understand the truths of the gospel only by the same process as they understand and comprehend them here. So when they hear the gospel preached in the spirit world, they will respond just as our fathers and mothers have, with a glad heart. They will love it and embrace it. It will then be easy to know who they are. They who have died without the knowledge of the truth, they who will receive it with glad hearts, they also will be candidates for celestial glory. When you die and go to the spirit world, you will labor for years, trying to convert individuals who will be taking their own course. Some of them will repent; some of them will listen. Another group will be rebellious, following their own will and notion, and that group will get smaller and smaller until every knee shall humbly bow and every tongue confess.

It may take us thousands of years to do that. But those who are of the blood of Israel, who had they been living, would have received the gospel and are not participators in the blessings, will in a similar manner receive it in the spirit world.

Now I want to go a little further and identify us and our posterity and our ancestors, to be able to tell you why it is that there is a great proportion of our Father's children who die without law and why you and I came into possession of the knowledge of the law. The Prophet Joseph Smith said-you will find these words in the fourth volume of Church History, page 231. This was at the time of the completion of the baptismal font in the Nauvoo Temple. The Prophet said:

"The Saints have the privilege of being baptized for those of their own relatives who are dead whom they believe would have embraced the gospel if they had lived, if they had had the privilege of hearing it, and who have received the gospel in the spirit world through the instrumentality of those who have been commissioned to preach to them while in prison."

The limitation given to Latter-day Saints at that time was, baptism for their dead whom they believe would have received the gospel. That is all. Now since we are not prepared to pass judgment on our dead ancestors whom we did not know, the Church has gone further and has permitted members of the Church to do the work for all their immediate ancestors unless they are murderers. There can be no work done for those who have committed murder.

Now, my brothers and sisters, I would like you to understand that long before we were born into this earth we were tested and tried in our pre-existence, and the fact that of the thousands of children born today, a certain proportion of them went to the Hottentots of South Africa; thousands went to the Chinese mothers; thousands went to Negro mothers; thousands to beautiful white Latter-day Saint mothers: You cannot tell me that the entire group was just designated, marked, to go where they did, that they were men and women of equal opportunities. There are no infant spirits born. They had a being ages before they came into this life. They appear in infant bodies, but they were tested, proven souls. Therefore, I say to you that long before we came into this life all groups and races of men existed as they exist today. Like attracts like.

Why is it in this Church we do not grant the priesthood to the Negroes? It is alleged that the Prophet Joseph said-and I have no reason to dispute it-that it is because of some act committed by them before they came into this life. It is alleged that they were neutral, standing neither for Christ nor the devil. But, I am convinced it is because of some things they did before they came into this life that they have been denied the privilege. The races of to-day are very largely reaping the consequence of a previous life.

That is why the Lord in giving Daniel the interpretation of that wonderful dream of Nebuchadnezzar was able to tell very clearly, long before they were born, when the various people should rise and bear rule upon the earth. There was a group of tested, tried, and proven souls before they were born into the world, and the Lord provided a lineage for them. That lineage is the house of Israel, the lineage of Abraham, Isaac, and Jacob, and their posterity. Through this lineage were to come the true and tried souls that had demonstrated their righteousness in the spirit world before they came here. We came through that lineage. Our particular branch is the house of Joseph through his son Ephraim. That is the group whence shall come the majority of the candidates for celestial glory. That is why we are doing the work for our ancestors and not for others.

LET us not imagine that in this dispensation we shall do the work for the dead Chinese or Hindus. I expect it will take one thousand years to complete in our temples the ordinances looking to the salvation of the house of Israel. It will take all Latter-day Saints and all that we can do to take care of our own branch-of our own house. While we do the work for our dead ancestors, we will reach a limit after a while. That limit will be after we have gone as far as records are kept. I have said that when any man or woman goes into this work earnestly, the Lord will provide ways and means for him to obtain the information he seeks. Our understanding will be opened and sources of knowledge will be made manifest. Why? Because the dead know a great deal more than we do about existing records.

Why is it that sometimes only one of a city or household receives the gospel? It was made known to me that it is because of the righteous dead who had received the gospel in the spirit world exercising themselves, and in answer to their prayers elders of the Church were sent to the homes of their posterity that the gospel might be taught to them, and through their righteousness they might be privileged to have a descendant in the flesh do the work for their dead kindred. I want to say to you that it is with greater intensity that the hearts of the fathers and mothers in the spirit world are turned to their children than that our hearts are turned to them.

And so it is that the Lord will open the way for those who seek information and knowledge.

I recall an incident in my own father's experience. How we looked forward to the completion of the Logan Temple! It was about to be dedicated. My father had labored on that house from its very beginning, and my earliest recollection was carrying his dinner each day as he brought the rock down from the quarry. How we looked forward to that great event! I remember how in the meantime Father made every effort to obtain all the data and information he could concerning his relatives. It was the theme of his prayer night and morning that the Lord would open the way whereby he could get information concerning his dead.

The day before the dedication while writing recommends to the members of his ward who were to be present at the first service, two elderly gentlemen walked down the streets of Logan, approached my two younger sisters, and, coming to the elder one of the two placed in her hands a newspaper and said:

"Take this to your father. Give it to no one else. Go quickly with it. Don't lose it."

The child responded and when she met her mother, her mother wanted the paper. The child said, "No, I must give it to Father and no one else."

She was admitted into the room and told her story. We looked in vain for these travelers. They were not to be seen. No one else saw them. Then we turned to the paper. The newspaper, The Newbury Weekly News, was printed in my father's old English home, Thursday, May 15th, 1884, and reached our hands May 18th, 1884, three days after its publication. We were astonished, for by no earthly means could it have reached us, so that our curiosity increased as we examined it. Then we discovered one page devoted to the writings of a reporter of the paper, who had gone on his vacation, and among other places had visited an old cemetery. The curious inscriptions led him to write what he found on the tombstones, including the verses. He also added the names, date of birth, death, etc., filling nearly an entire page.

It was the old cemetery where the Ballard family had been buried for generations, and very many of my father's immediate relatives and other intimate friends were mentioned.

When the matter was presented to President Merrill of the Logan Temple, he said, "You are authorized to do the work for those because you received it through messengers of the Lord."

There is no doubt that the dead who had received the gospel in the spirit world had put it into the heart of that reporter to write these things, and thus the way was prepared for my father to obtain the information he sought, and so with you who are earnest in this work, the way shall be opened and you will be able to gather data far beyond your expectations. I will tell you what will happen. When you have gone as far as you can go, the names of your righteous dead who have embraced the gospel in the spirit world will be given you through the instrumentality of your dead kindred. But only the names of those who have received the gospel will be revealed.

Now, I wish to say to you that those who died without law, meaning the pagan nations, for lack of faithfulness, for lack of devotion, in the former life, are obtaining all that they are entitled to. I don't mean to say that all of them will be barred from entrance into the highest glory. Any one of them who repents and complies with the conditions might also obtain celestial glory, but the great bulk of them will only obtain terrestrial glory.

Any man or woman, not only those in the days of Noah, who heard the gospel and rejected it, but in this day any man or woman who has had a good chance to have heard the gospel, to receive it and embrace it and enjoy its blessings and privileges, who lived during their life in absolute indifference to these things, ignoring it, and neglected it, need not hope or anticipate that when he is dead the work can be done for him and he gain celestial glory. Don't you Latter-day Saints get the notion that a man or woman can live in defiance or total indifference, having had a good chance-not a casual chance or opportunity-and when they die, you can go and do the work for that individual and have them receive every blessing that the faithful ones are entitled to. If that becomes the doctrine of the Church we will be worse than the Catholics, who believe that you can pray a man out of purgatory. But they charge for it, and we don't, so we would be more foolish than they.

I say this to stimulate you to try and make your lives conform to the commandments of the Master, that you may work while the day lasts, for the night cometh when it will not profit a man to work. That applies to those who had a chance to receive the gospel but rejected it. I want to say this: It applies also to men and women who neglect going to the house of God, who think, "Oh, well, if I don't do the work, my wife will fix it up." I tell you they are treading on dangerous ground. They may wake up and find that their day and opportunity have gone. They had the chance; they died without accepting it. They neglected it and may lose it.

I am not judging their case: the Lord will judge every case on its merits.

"These are they who are honorable men of the earth, who were blinded by the craftiness of men.

"These are they who receive of his glory, but not of his fulness.

"These are they who receive of the presence of the Son, but not of the fulnes of the Father.

"Wherefore, they are bodies terrestrial and not bodies celestial, and differ in glory as the moon differs from the sun.

"These are they who are not valiant in the testimony of Jesus; wherefore, they obtain not the crown over the kingdom of our God." (Ibid. 75-79.)

There are Latter-day Saints, many of them, who are not valiant in the testimony of Jesus, though they have entered into these covenants have not kept them. They have broken their pledges and may come forth in the resurrection and find themselves wholly unworthy to be candidates for the celestial glory. They will come up in the terrestrial world. It is for us to make our calling and election sure. We can do it in this life.

Now let me pass to the third and last of these groups, the telestial.

"And again, we saw the glory of the telestial, which glory is that of the lesser, even as the glory of the stars differ from that of the glory of the moon in the firmament.

"These are they who received not the gospel of Christ, neither the testimony of Jesus.

"These are they who deny the Holy Spirit.

"These are they who are thrust down to hell.

"These are they who shall not be redeemed from the devil until the last resurrection, until the Lord, even Christ the Lamb, shall have finished his work.

"These are they who receive not of his fulness in the eternal world, but of the Holy Spirit through the ministration of the terrestrial;

"And the terrestrial through the ministration of the celestial.

"And also the telestial receive it of the administering of angels who are appointed to minister for them, or who are appointed to be ministering spirits for them; for they shall be heirs of salvation.

"And thus we saw, in the heavenly vision, the glory of the telestial, which surpasses all understanding;

"And no man knows it except him to whom God has revealed it.

"And thus we saw the glory of the terrestrial, which excels in all things the glory of the telestial, even in glory, and in power, and might, and in dominion.

"And thus we saw the glory of the celestial, which excels in all things-where God, even the Father, reigns upon his throne forever and ever;

"Before whose throne all things bow in humble reverence and give him glory forever and ever.

"They who dwell in his presence are the church of the Firstborn, and they see as they are seen, and know as they are known, having received of his fulness and of his grace;

"And he makes them equal in power, and in might, and in dominion.

"And the glory of the celestial is one, even as the glory of the sun is one.

"And the glory of the terrestrial is one, even as the glory of the moon is one.

"And the glory of the telestial is one, even as the glory of the stars is one; for as one star differs from another star in glory, even so differs one from another in glory in the telestial world;

"For these are they who are of Paul, and of Apollos, and of Cephas.

"These are they who say they are some of one and some of another-some of Christ and some of John, and some of Moses, and some of Elias, and some of Esaias, and some of Isaiah, and some of Enoch;

"But received not the gospel, neither the testimony of Jesus, neither the prophets, neither the everlasting covenant.

"Last of all, these are they who will not be gathered with the saints, to be caught up unto the church of the Firstborn, and received into the cloud.

"These are they who are liars, and sorcerers, and adulterers, and whoremongers, and whosoever loves and makes a lie.

"These are they who suffer the wrath of God on the earth.

"These are they who suffer the vengeance of eternal fire.

"These are they who are cast down to hell and suffer the wrath of Almighty God, until the fulness of times when Christ shall have subdued all enemies under his feet, and shall have perfected his work;

"When he shall deliver up the kingdom, and present it unto the father, spotless, saying: I have overcome and have trodden the wine-press alone, even the wine-press of the fierceness of the wrath of Almighty God.

"Then shall he be crowned with the crown of his glory, to sit on the throne of his power to reign forever and ever.

"But behold, and lo, we saw the glory and the inhabitants of the telestial world, that they were as innumerable as the stars in the firmament of heaven, or as the sand upon the seashore,

"And heard the voice of the Lord, saying: These all shall bow the knee, and every tongue shall confess to him who sits upon the throne forever and ever;

"For they shall be judged according to their works, and every man shall receive according to his own works, his own dominion, in the mansions which are prepared;

"And they shall be servants of the Most High; but where God and Christ dwell they cannot come, worlds without end." (Ibid. 81-112.)

NOW I wish to answer one or two queries that undoubtedly have arisen in your minds, and in doing so I wish to read some more scripture. The question is often asked, "Is it possible for one who attains telestial glory in time in the eternal world to live so well that he may graduate from the telestial and pass into the terrestrial, and then after a season that he may progress from that and be ultimately worthy of the celestial glory?" That is the query that has been asked. I have just read the answer, so far as the telestial group is concerned. "Where God and Christ dwell they cannot come, worlds without end." I take it upon the same basis, the same argument likewise applies to the terrestrial world. Those whose lives have entitled them to terrestrial glory can never gain celestial glory. One who gains possession of the lowest degree of the telestial glory may ultimately arise to the highest degree of that glory, but no provision has been made for promotion from one glory to another. Let us be reasonable about it.

I wish to say in illustrating the subject that if three men were starting out on an endless race, one having an advantage of one mile, the other of two miles, and each one could run as fast as the other, when would the last ever catch up to the first? If you can tell me that, I can tell you when candidates for the telestial glory will get into the celestial glory. Each will grow, but his development will be prescribed by his environment, and there is a reason for it.

Applying this illustration to those who are entitled to the different degrees of glory: He who enters the celestial glory has the advantage over all others. He dwells in the presence of the Father and the Son. His teachers are the highest. The others will receive all they learn from the celestial to the terrestrial, from the terrestrial to the telestial. They get it second hand and third hand, and how can they ever hope to grow as fast as those who drink from the fountainhead? Again those who come forth in the celestial glory with celestial bodies have a body that is more refined. It is different. The very fibre and texture of the celestial body is more pure and holy than a telestial or terrestrial body, and a celestial body alone can endure celestial glory. I am impressed with this because I recall when a child at school I learned that if an icicle a mile square were dropped into the sun it would melt in an instant, and when I learned how intense the heat of that orb is and that our sun is a celestial world, I did not know whether I wanted to live in a celestial world or not if it was that hot. But when I come to understand, if I have a body suitable to dwell in eternal burnings, then I think I would like it. Fish can live in the water and have bodies suited to that element but entirely unsuitable to a life outside of the water. When we have a celestial body, it will be suited to the celestial conditions, and a telestial body could not endure celestial glory. It would be torment and affliction to them. I have not read in the scripture where there will be another resurrection where we can obtain a celestial body for a terrestrial body.

What we receive in the resurrection will be ours forever and forever.

I have several times been asked, how is it possible for those who attain celestial glory ever to feel fully happy and satisfied to know that their children are in the telestial world, and never would have the privilege of coming up with their parents in the celestial kingdom.

We must not overlook the fact that those who attain to the higher glories may minister unto and visit and associate with those of the lesser kingdoms. While the lesser may not come up, they may still enjoy the companionship of their loved ones who are in higher stations. Also we must not forget that even the least degree of glory, as the Lord has expressed it, is beyond all our present understanding. So that they are in the presence of glorious conditions, even though they attain unto the least place, and we must not forget either that these, our sons, are our Father's sons and daughters; and he has other sons and daughters who do not even attain unto the telestial kingdom. They are sons of perdition out with the devil and his angels, and though the Father has grieved over them, he still has not the power to rescue and save them because he gave them free agency, and they used that in such a manner that they have shut themselves out from his presence. But he is justified. He has performed his full duty by them and that is the condition which we ought to be in to feel justified, though we may be so unfortunate as to have some of our own children in the lesser kingdoms, if we have done our full duty by them. We may be sad at the thought of their not being with us, but we will not have the sting or remorse of conscience. If we have failed, however, to do our duty, then naturally we will feel to regret their situation and censure ourselves in part for the same.

Let me read to you from the 88th section, commencing with the 17th verse:

"And the redemption of the soul is through him who quickeneth all things, in whose bosom it is decreed that the poor and the meek of the earth shall inherit it.

"Therefore, it must needs be sanctified from all unrighteousness, that it may be prepared for the celestial glory." (Ibid. 88:17.)

This earth, every part of it, will be celestial; not one-third telestial, and one-third terrestrial. It will be celestial-and only celestial beings shall dwell upon it. I always thought the Lord would require a larger would than ours for the telestial bodies to dwell on when I consider the millions of dead who will inherit the telestial glory. They may need some planet bigger than this earth.

Let me read again:

"Wherefore, it shall be sanctified; yea, notwithstanding it shall die, it shall be quickened and the righteous shall inherit it.

"For notwithstanding they die, they also shall rise again, a spiritual body.

"They who are of a celestial spirit shall receive the same body which was a natural body; even ye shall receive your bodies, and your glory shall be that glory by which your bodies are quickened.

"Ye who are quickened by a portion of the celestial glory shall then receive of the same, even a fulness.

"And they who are quickened by a portion of the terrestrial glory shall then receive of the same, even a fulness.

"And also they who are quickened by a portion of the telestial glory shall then receive of the same, even a fulness." (Ibid. 26-31.)

Therefore, I say, my brothers and sisters, the Lord has distinctly settled the question of our status, as established in our resurrection from the dead. If we have earned a celestial body, we may have celestial glory. Yet many of the Saints will wake up and find they sold their birthright for a mess of pottage. If I should come forth and find myself in the telestial world, or in the terrestrial world, and look up to this earth, when it shall attain its place as a celestial orb, shining like a sun, when this earth will no longer need the sun to shine upon it by day nor the moon by night, when it shall become a sun, if I should be so unfortunate as to lose my chance of obtaining an inheritance in that place, and be compelled to dwell upon a telestial orb, I surely will feel the full force of the poet's statement, "Of all sad words of tongue and pen, the saddest are these, it might have been." I might have been there. I was born there. It was my right and privilege to be there, but I lost it through my own blindness, through my own wickedness; I have lost it forever. While I might have joy here, and experience and growth here, yet I have lost eternal companionship with my Heavenly Father.

Let me not only appeal to you to be greatly interested in working out the salvation of your dead, but be also intensely interested, be deeply concerned in the salvation of the living. What mortification, what humiliation would it be for me to stand before my redeemed dead, for whom I have labored in the temples, and have them say to me, "What of your sons or your daughters, your grandsons or granddaughters, those born under the covenants, born in the most glorious Dispensation of the Fulness of Times, yet were so foolish as to lose their right to the enjoyment of celestial glory?" How great would be my mortification and humiliation! And yet, there are great numbers of our children and our acquaintances, with whom we are now associated, who are in danger of losing their eternal salvation in the celestial kingdom of our God. While there is life, let us earnestly labor with all our might, mind, and strength that we may bring them to Christ in full possession of all these blessings. And we can do it. Even if we labor all our lives, we shall have great joy if we save but one, for we will be shedding an influence for good over countless thousands who shall be their posterity. But if we have not done our full duty, we shall sorrow intensely because of our neglect, and we shall stand accused by them for having failed in the performance of our duty. On the other hand, if we have labored with all our might, mind, and strength, we shall stand with a clear conscience, blameless. Our status and condition will be like our Heavenly Father's. He sent his Only Begotten Son to save and redeem mankind, but unless we accept the atonement and act in conformity to the laws and requirements laid down for us, even God cannot save us.

Let us not be discouraged in our temple work. Let us renew our diligence and determination to do this work, and what we do not understand concerning our sealings, it will be later revealed to us.

You mothers worry about your little children. We do not perform sealings for them. I lost a son six years of age, and I saw him a man in the spirit world after his death, and I saw how he had exercised his own freedom of choice and would obtain of his own will and volition a companionship, and in due time to him, and all

29

those who are worthy of it, shall come all of the blessings and sealing privileges of the house of the Lord. Do not worry over it. They are safe; they are all right.

Now, then, what of your daughters who have died and have not been sealed to some man? Unless it is made known to you, let their case rest. They will make known to you the agreements and contracts they have mutually entered into. The sealing power shall be forever and ever with this Church, and provisions will be made for them. We cannot run faster than the Lord has provided the way. Their blessings and privileges will come to them in due time. In the meantime, they are safe.

Let us be earnest in this work. It will cast an influence over your whole families. It will strengthen your faith. It will add testimony to your faith. Surely there is peace and joy in it. May you find it, and may everyone under the sound of my voice, go hence with a firm resolve, such as we have never had before, that we will make our calling and election sure, that at the last day our records may be clear, that there may be no clouds upon our titles, that we may receive our inheritance in the celestial glory of our God. If that shall be our reward, our joy will be full, beyond all my power to tell you. May the Lord help us to have a clear conscience and to do every day that which we ought to do. I am more concerned for the living than for the dead, when I realize that when the bridegroom cometh, five, or one-half, of the virgins shall be asleep, without oil in their lamps. That will not be the world; that will be the Latter-day Saints. Will you be asleep, or will there be oil in your lamps? Let us stand in our places and not flatter ourselves by thinking, "I will take care of John and Mary when they are dead." Let us not procrastinate but labor unceasingly for the salvation of our kindred, and if we succeed, if we win that prize, we shall be compensated beyond all expectations. We shall receive more than we have ever dreamed of joy and happiness and eternal satisfaction, but if we miss it, if we lose it, we, whose right it is to obtain it, I cannot tell you the sting of conscience and remorse, the hell of torment we shall endure endlessly, if we miss it, through our own ignorance and foolishness. May God save us from that affliction.

The Lord sanctify these humble remarks and my earnest testimony and desire for your blessing and welfare, for the salvation of the living and the dead, I pray in the name of Jesus Christ. Amen.

Personnel Lists

NORTH WEBER STAKE GENEALOGICAL COMMITTEE

PERSONNEL

CHARLES KINGSTON, Stake Representative
LEVI J. TAYLOR
JOHN FELT
JAS. L. ROBSOX
LEANDER HARRIS
JULIA PARRY
MARY P. KINGSTON
MRS. CUNNINGHAM

WEBER STAKE GENEALOGICAL COMMITTEE

PERSONNEL

D. R. ROBERTS, Stake Representative
JOHN T. BURNETT
JESSE A. CHILDS
JESSE N. STEPHENS
JOSEPH PATTERSON
GEORGE C. HOBSON
HERBERT BURRELL
MARGARET P. BINGHAM
MAUDE JONES
ETHEL SKELTON

OGDEN STAKE GENEALOGICAL COMMITTEE

PERSONNEL

THOMAS CLARK, Stake Representative
GEO. A. SEAMON
ELLEN B. COWLES
HARRY M. WELLS
ELMER J. LARSON
HENRY B. THOMPSON
ELIZABETH Y. THOMPSON
LOUISE NELSON
GEORGE A. FULLER

The Slogan of the Four Ogden City Stakes is:

"A Temple for Ogden and Soon."

Mount Ogden Stake Presidency

ROBERT I. BURTON
JOSEPH RIRIE
JOSEPH C. MCFARLANE

High Council:

M. CHAS. WOODS
ALFRED GLADWELL
MARTIN DALEBOUT
HYRUM A. SHUPE
WM. H. REEDER, JR.
JOS. E. EVANS
WM. S. PAINE
A. LEON WINDSOR
WILFORD O. RIDGES
JAMES W. URE
CHRISTOPHER J. BROWN
J. P. CORRY
EVERT NEUTEBOOM
WM. BARNES
EGBERT STRATFORD
WM. Z. TERRY, STAKE CLERK

Mount Ogden Stake Slogan:

"A Temple Worker in Every Home and a Temple for Ogden."